One Great TRAIN RIDE

By Jessiey James

Illustrations by Carolyn Mottern

To order additional copies of this book, contact:
Xlibris
844-714-8691
www.Xlibris.com
Orders@Xlibris.com

ISBN: 978-1-6641-6182-5 (sc)
ISBN: 978-1-6641-6183-2 (hc)
ISBN: 978-1-6641-6181-8 (e)

Print information available on the last page

Rev. date: 03/11/2021

DEDICATION

To my son:
Brandon

Me and my parents, Jessie and Robbie, jump in our gray car. We are traveling a couple hours away. We are going to meet up with my grandparents

First we are to stop at a museum to see a safe that once belonged to my mom's family. It was stolen in "The Great Bennett Safe Robbery of 1868". They got it back. It is now in the museum place.

Second we are to take a ride
on an old train. It is called the
A B and C. My mom packed us
a lunch to eat on the train.

3

As soon as we arrive at the museum, a Tour Guide takes us to the room where the safe is on display. My mom is disappointed. The safe isn't any larger than a large box.

My mom remarks: "Wow, this is so small." The Tour Guide says: "It may look small, but is very heavy." I think I heard her say it weighs 320 pounds. I loved seeing the safe in the museum. Too bad I can't play with it.

MUSEUM

TOUR GUIDE

The Tour Guide already knew we were coming
to see the safe that was in my mom's family.
She then leads us into another room and has a
bunch of papers for my mom. They have pictures
on them of the safe, people and a house.

As we are walking out of the room, the Tour Guide remarks to my mom: "Our museum would be very grateful if you were to write a small book about the safe and some of your family history. We are in need of books to see here at the Museum." My mom is surprised.

My mom has information that a Bennett married a distant relative in our family. This family claims that their family, specifically, John Bennett, was really the first to discover oil but another family got all the credit.

8

Next we walk over to ride the train. A blue train is down the tracks. As soon as the blue train stops, we notice my Grandparents getting off. I am so excited to see them. We exchange hugs.

Pa Pa says: "We came early and already rode the train." And yes, they loved the ride. We hardly get to talk to them. It is time to get on the train for our ride. I can't wait.

I sit by the window. The blue train goes by lots of woods and trees. The train rocks and rolls. It is very slow. Riders on the train are allowed to walk around inside the train cars. We are also allowed to go from one train car to another. Train Lady says kids have to stay with parents. No running.

11

We eat our lunch on the train.
I am watching out the window.
Oh look, there is a deer. I think
it sees me.

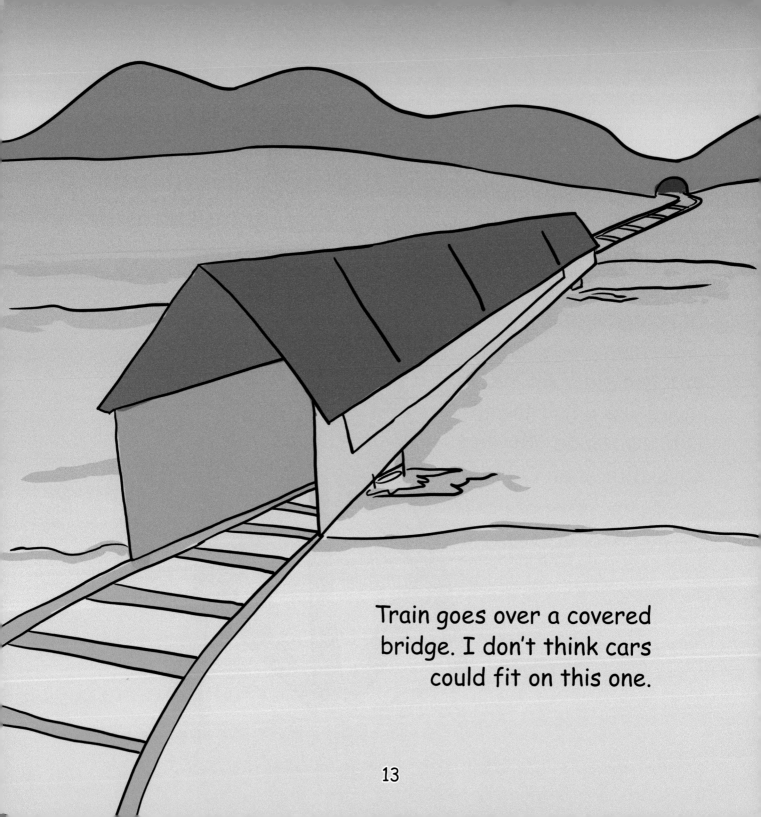

Train goes over a covered bridge. I don't think cars could fit on this one.

Along the ride, there are a couple places that have decorations set up. The Train Lady points out two places. One looks like a cell tower. It is brown wood. My dad says that is an Oil Rig.

Another place has people dressed up in big clothes and a wagon. My dad says that is a Stagecoach.

My dad can't believe how much the train rolls. He says: "I wonder if other trains run like this too?" I saw a kids train on display once at a place near our house. This blue train is much larger than that one.

16

This train ride is making me very sleepy.
I fall asleep. I have a dream:

I dream I am riding a train. Bad guys stopped the train. They climbed aboard. They opened a black safe that was in the baggage car. They took money out. We all had to step out of the train. The bad guys took off with the train. They left us.

I wake up crying. My mother hugs me. Then, we talk about my real first train ride. There were lots of trees and water. There were no bad guys. It was just some bad guys that stole the safe. And it was the one on display at the museum. And that was a long time ago. This was just a dream.

My mother then ask: "Do you remember what you did today?"
I say: "First went to see the safe. Second rode my first
train. And it was ONE GREAT TRAIN RIDE!"

19

T0143981

Printed in the United States
by Baker & Taylor Publisher Services